Arne Jacobsen
A Danish architect

D1743885

Born in Copenhagen on 11 February 1902.
Died in Copenhagen on 3 March 1971.
Educated at the Royal Academy of
Fine Arts, School of Architecture,
in Copenhagen. Diploma 1927.
Professor 1956-1965.
Eckersberg Medal 1936.
Prize of Honour,
São Paulo Biennale, 1954.
C. F. Hansen Medal 1955.
Grand Prix Internationale
d'Architecture 1960.
Medal of Honour,
Danish Architectural Association, 1962.
Honorary Corresponding Member of the
Royal British Institute of Architects 1963.
Member of Akademie der Künste,
Berlin, 1964.
Member of Academie Nazionale
de San Luca, 1965.
Member of Académie Serbe des Sciences
et des Arts, Belgrade, 1965.
Honorary Doctor, Oxford University, 1966.
Die Plakette der Akademie der Künste,
Hamburg, 1969.
Medaille d'Or, Academie d'Architecture
de France, 1971.

PRESENTATION BOOKS MINISTRY OF FOREIGN AFFAIRS COPENHAGEN

Arne Jacobsen
By Poul Erik Skriver

Poul Erik Skriver is one of the best known Danish writers on architecture. An architect himself, he is head of the Danish Architectural Press and editor of the magazines 'Arkitektur' (Architecture) and 'Arkitekten' (The Architect).

Functionalism made its first impact in Scandinavia in about 1930. The pioneers had difficulty in the late 1920's in illustrating the new ideas – owing to a shortage of far-sighted clients. It was the building exhibitions that broke the ice. The Stockholm exhibition of 1930, with Gunnar Asplund as the chief architect, was of special importance. In Denmark it was a smaller building exhibition in 1929 which presented the new architectural ideal to a general public. Arne Jacobsen in association with Flemming Lassen had designed a show house which broke entirely with the traditional conception of a villa. The house was purely for display, being erected in a large hall as a dummy and intended to stand for a few weeks only.

This 'House of the Future' with a brief lifetime is of great historic interest because it tells such a lot about the development of functionalism, in which it was the design ideal and not the social ideas of functionalism that emerged first. A characteristic work of this pioneer period is Rothenborg House, a villa built for a well-to-do family north of Copenhagen. The first works of Le Corbusier and Mies van der Rohe also were individual houses. Rothenborg House, which was typical of the cubist ideals of early functionalism, has since been completely altered.

With the artist's intuition, Arne Jacobsen saw that a settlement with the surface historicism and dogmatic classicism of the past was necessary in order to pave the way for progress in other sectors of building also. But it was a process which took many years and saw many reverses. Designing individual houses for the comfortable middle class was an important activity especially for young architects, including Arne Jacobsen. It was difficult to persuade conservative builders to accept the new ideas; and so many of his houses of this period are strongly influenced by Danish building traditions, though more freely designed to fit the purpose instead of being determined by dogmatic concepts of style.

Jacobsen participated throughout his life in numerous architectural competitions, as a rule successfully. He had a knack of finding a simple and logical solution to even a complex project. In the competitive design he demonstrated that the new architectural ideals usually led to more appropriate solutions than traditional architectural designs, and he had a marked talent for illustrating his ideas. He obtained some of his most important commissions through these competitions. In 1932 he won a closed competition for a planned beach development at Bellevue, north of Copenhagen. A horse-riding hall designed by him had already been built in this area in 1930. In 1934 he designed the Bella Vista apartment houses at Bellevue, and in 1935 the Bellevue Theatre and attached restaurant, also by him, were built. He thus came to dominate the whole new environment which grew up near to the old Klampenborg railway station, ten kilometres north of Copenhagen, a popular excursion area with Copenhageners for many generations.

It was to be of vital importance to the emergence of modernism in Denmark that the new ideas were presented with such charm and talent at a place frequented by tens of thousands of people. The beach at Bellevue became almost a symbol of the new age of free bathing in gay and festive surroundings.

The housing development of Bella Vista was to remain for many years the ideal design for apartment blocks. Emancipated from the traditional ideas of closed courtyards, Jacobsen had exploited the site's attractions: old trees and a view of the Sound. The two angles of the development opened out to the sun and the view, the buildings being designed so as

to allow each apartment a share in the treats. Large balconies gave an open-air extension and big corner windows provided an outlook. All the main principles of functionalism had here been fulfilled. But circumstances in Denmark, as in most other countries, meant that the new housing ideals were reserved for a narrow circle of the well-to-do. The new ideas penetrated only slowly into social building.

A distinctive feature of Arne Jacobsen's work is the care with which every detail is designed to support the whole. He saw a building as a physical setting for the life to be lived there, and he considered furniture and fittings, floor and wall materials, lighting and window details to be just as important as the building's general design and outward appearance. It was not his wish to dominate this environment or decide for others, but to serve them with his knowledge and his art and so make their life easier and fuller.

One of the first projects he was able to design in the light of this ideal was a small commercial building, Stelling House, in the old town in Copenhagen. The house stands on the corner of an old street of unpretentious neo-classicist domestic buildings and with a short front overlooking Gammel Torv, the old town square containing commercial buildings from various periods. Stelling House was the first modernistic house to be built in the old town; new development up to then had taken the form of pastiche, in a mistaken desire to fit in with the old. The building gave rise to violent public debate, with protests and polemics against 'inconsiderate' treatment of an old civic environment.

Today the building is accepted by everyone as an outstanding example of considerate adjustment of modernism to an existing earlier development. The house is made to fit in with its surroundings in proportions and treatment of materials. The two lower storeys contain a shop for painters' requisites and artists' materials. All fittings were designed by Jacobsen. Here he created one of the finest shop interiors in Copenhagen.

In the immediate pre-war years Arne Jacobsen, in association with Erik Møller, won a competition for a town hall at Århus in Jutland; and in association with Flemming Lassen, the competition for a town hall at Søllerød, north of Copenhagen. Both buildings are characteristic of the modified functionalism which presumably was a result of political developments in Europe. The pioneers of functionalism in Germany had been silenced; most of them emigrated to Britain and the United States. Le Corbusier also had difficulty in prevailing with his ideas. There had been a trend towards consolidation of national traditions.

The two town hall designs, and especially the Søllerød one, were inspired by the Swedish architect Gunnar Asplund whom Jacobsen admired for the artistic assurance with which he had interpreted modernism; in the extension to the town hall at Gothenburg, for example.

National self-absorption increased at the outbreak of the Second World War and the German occupation of Denmark. It was to affect the work of every architect, Arne Jacobsen not excepted. In 1943 he designed a herring smokehouse at Odden harbour, a small fishing village in northwest Zealand. But even here, in this national-romantic work, he revealed his masterly skill in expressing a building's function architecturally.

In 1943 Arne Jacobsen had for political reasons to leave Denmark and settle temporarily as a refugee in Sweden. At that time, in collaboration with his wife, Jonna Jacobsen, a textile printer, he had begun to experiment with silk-printed textiles. Alongside his architectural work, he had continuously practised visual art, mostly

"The House of the Future", erected at a building exhibition in Copenhagen, 1929. This project was carried out by Arne Jacobsen in collaboration with Flemming Lassen.

in the form of watercolours. He was a fine connoisseur of Danish flora. Through his watercolours he studied characteristic plant environments; the forest floor, salt marshes, wayside ditches, etc. He stylized these motifs into textile designs, but with respect for naturalistic veracity in the rendering of individual plants. In Sweden he was able to continue with these experiments, and a production of curtain materials and wallpapers was started. They achieved great popularity and gave rise to a whole new epoch, with numerous imitations in Sweden and Denmark.

When Jacobsen returned to Denmark immediately after the war, Danish building was marred by shortages of materials and the depression of the occupation. He got started, however, relatively quickly on some minor housing developments, seeking to overcome restrictions on materials and national wartime narrow-mindedness by designing the buildings in large, simple features, in an almost anonymous modernism; for example, in the youth housing project at Gentofte from 1947 and a terrace-house development from 1951. But once again it was to be in the area round Bellevue that he would manifest a turning-point in his development. Not far from Bella Vista, he had the opportunity to develop a former country estate with a number of individual linked and terraced houses. Søholm, as this small development is called, aroused immense interest, also internationally. It was publicized in architectural journals all over the world. What were the qualities which made this unassuming development so admired? There can scarcely be any explanation other than that it is an architectural masterpiece, in which the artist's temperament and complete command of his medium have created a building environment of rare beauty. The whole is harmonized by a well-calculated rhythm in the staggering of the individual houses. Everything is proportioned with assurance, every detail designed meticulously as under- and overtones of the suggested main theme.

The planting of the site with old trees, ground displacements, proximity to the coast and the linking of the individual houses have been employed in the design of a very rich close environment. There are screened and sheltered garden areas; in the common area at the entrance side of the houses a luxuriant and very varied plant environment has grown up.

Arne Jacobsen is sometimes described as a gifted interpreter of the great pioneers, Le Corbusier and especially Mies van der Rohe. Indications of this may be found, but in most of his works, and especially in Søholm, he displays an originality, an entirely individual conception of design, which embraces the overall environment. He equipped one of the houses as a home for himself and his family, creating here environments which clearly contradicted the widespread view of Jacobsen as a cool and severe functionalist. The garden, designed and planted by himself, contained several hundred species of plants, planted with a connoisseur's and an artist's understanding of the laws of plant ecology. The luxuriance reappears in the rooms, where, on walls and shelves, are specimens of beautifully designed applied art from many countries and many periods.

Arne Jacobsen's concern for the quality of environment, whether of home or of work, found convincing expression in Munkegaard School, built for Gentofte municipality, north of Copenhagen, in 1952-56. With a view to the practical functions and comprehensiveness, the plan is clearcut and almost schematic. The general classrooms are in single-storey buildings, separated by small

Rothenborg House in Ordrup, north of Copenhagen, 1930.

garden courtyards. Science and technical classrooms, administration and staff rooms are in a two-storey wing. In the middle of the layout is a large assembly hall. The classrooms are designed so as to be well lit and well ventilated, conducive to a pleasant indoor climate. Classrooms and corridors all have windows opening on to garden courtyards, all planted differently, and with such characteristic differences of plant types and design that each class section acquires a separate identity. To go about the school is like walking in a large garden with many summer-houses.

The wartime shortages of materials only began to ease in the 1950's. Meanwhile, intensified building needs all over Europe had promoted an interest in industrialized building methods. The traditional forms of building and the traditional Danish building material, brick, were considered an unsuitable basis for industrialization. Mass production called for modular planning as a preliminary to employment of prefabricated building components. Arne Jacobsen saw industrialization of the building process as a necessary means to increasing the volume of building as well as a way of cheapening it in the long run. But it needed a new approach, the acquirement of a new design idiom. Gropius and Mies van der Rohe, already in the 1920's, had foreseen and theoretically discussed a future industrialization of building, and in the United States had found opportunities for working on these possibilities in practice. They had formed a school, and a number of gifted Americans, on the basis of these ideas, had developed the curtain-wall principle. Familiar buildings were those of Eero Saarinen for General Motors' research centre in Detroit, and Skidmore, Owings and Merrill's Lever House in New York. Inspired not least by these works, Jacobsen designed two buildings in which, starting out from his own axioms, he elaborated the design problems to be solved before any industrialization could be started. The buildings can perhaps best be described as craft-produced prototypes for later industrialization.

The first is Rødovre Town Hall, an administration building for a Copenhagen outer suburb. It was inaugurated in 1955. There is an obvious similarity with Eero Saarinen's buildings for General Motors, but in its proportioning, detail and internal design it is a characteristic Jacobsen work.

The building's load-bearing structures are of reinforced concrete, many of the components being prefabricated. The supporting pillars are centrally placed in the building, the outer walls being a non-bearing structure of slender steel sections and glass, a curtain wall suspended from the front edges of the reinforced concrete floors.

The other project is the SAS Royal Hotel and air terminal, built near the centre of Copenhagen in 1958-60. This bears a faint resemblance to Skidmore, Owing and Merrill's Lever House, but by this time Jacobsen had so completely emancipated himself from the American models for his own designing to be fully decisive to the building's architectural quality. In this design also the load-bearing structures are reinforced concrete, the facades being a light curtain-wall construction. With its eighteen storeys, the building is one of the few tower structures in central Copenhagen. It was Jacobsen's wish that it should not dwarf the surroundings by its great volume; he therefore wanted, through choice of materials, colours and detailing, to give to it the airiness of a mirage. Less than half of the facade is windows, but the high window surrounds are clad with glass in a grey-blue colour. The facades reflect the sky and drifting clouds, and the building has really achieved the desired lightness. The low-

Stelling House, Copenhagen, 1937-38.

rise wing which contains the terminal was made deliberately heavier, in colour and material, in order to draw attention from the tall building.

Everything in this building was designed by Arne Jacobsen, interiors, materials and colours of floors, walls and ceiling, lighting, curtains and carpets, furniture, ashtrays, etc. Thus a unique entity has been created, in a hotel environment where rooms with quite different functions have acquired a mutual relationship.

The problem was solved in a way characteristic of Jacobsen. The furniture and other objects designed specially for this hotel were generalized, thus enabling them to be used under many different conditions. In designing each object he took account of the possibility of mass production. Much of his furniture, many textiles and other articles that are now known and marketed all over the world were conceived in this way. For the Royal Hotel, for instance, he designed the two famous chairs, the Egg and the Swan.

Arne Jacobsen, however, has also designed furniture, textiles and other things for industry direct. Probably his most famous chair is the three-legged stacking chair of 1952, designed for the firm of Fritz Hansen's Eftf. This is a distinctly industrial product, the seat and back consisting of one piece of moulded plywood, the legs of tubular steel. In 1955, for the same firm he designed a four-legged chair on the identical constructive principle. This chair has been developed with variants on the same basic design for various uses, in restaurants, auditoria, churches, etc. There are not many countries in the world where it will not be found.

Another characteristic work, designed with the same fitness for practical use and industrial mass production, is a set of cutlery of stainless steel, executed for A. Michelsen, court jewellers, in 1957, together with jugs and other tableware, also in stainless steel, made for the firm Stelton A/S. By means of designs which render them suitable for industrial production, these articles can be made in qualities and with a finish corresponding to those of craft-produced objects, but at far lower prices. In his work on utensils, Jacobsen achieved the application of industrialization that had also been his aim in building.

From the late 1950's Arne Jacobsen was greatly concerned with the potentialities of component building. He set himself to clarifying building forms, in order that the work of building might take the form of assembling prefabricated components but with retention of architectural quality. Characteristic here is Toms Chocolate factory of 1961. It was built in prefabricated concrete components, which can be dismantled and re-erected in any extension of the factory.

In the early 1960's Jacobsen participated actively in a number of major architectural competitions and in design projects abroad. One of his last large-scale commissions, the head office of the Hamburg electricity works, was gained through an international competition in 1962. His associate, and later partner, in this work was Otto Weitling.

The building, opened for use in 1970, stands in a quarter of Hamburg which is reserved for office buildings, and where it is a condition that an architectural competition must be held for every new one. Perhaps for this reason many of the buildings have an obtrusive design, an exaggerated individuality. It is as if they are trying to compete for attention. In contrast, Jacobsen's is a very simple, almost anonymous structure; yet, because of its large and full features, it is the most conspicuous of them all. The monolithic, inhuman nature of large office buildings Jacobsen sought to compensate for in the design of the interiors of the low building which forms a sort of base for the tall one. Here are the general offices and public facilities, canteens, meeting-rooms and a lecture hall. These interiors, frequented by many people, have been made cheerful with colours, conservatories and varying light and material effects.

Another of Arne Jacobsen's great international commissions was St. Catherine's College, Oxford. It was awarded to him after the building committee had spent some time travelling in order to study works by a number of well-known architects. The committee, and especially its chairman, Mr. Alan Bullock, Master of St. Catherine's, were convinced that Arne Jacobsen could create both a human and a distinctive environment.

The architectural designing of a building results from a great many factors, most of them quite locally determined. A college at Oxford is based on very old traditions, the college buildings being grouped round a quadrangle and its area clearly limited and defined. This area includes living quarters for students and staff as well as teaching rooms. The lifestyle at a college is determined by old traditions, which make particular demands on the mutual siting and designing of the rooms; for example, the dining hall has other functions besides purely material ones. Certain symbolic values attach to it which can be difficult for foreigners to appreciate.

The site is on the outskirts of Oxford by a small stream and near some extensive meadows, while the old colleges lie close together in an urban environment. In these circumstances, Jacobsen elected to base his design on a classical ideal: a symmetrical, well-balanced building layout with a central quadrangle as in the traditional college. Otherwise, however, the buildings are in a completely contemporary idiom, the individual buildings corresponding in design and char-

Århus Town Hall, designed in collaboration with Erik Møller, 1939-42.

Fish smokehouse, Odden Harbour, 1943.
Fabric print from the early 1940's.

Youth residences in Gentofte, 1947.

acter to their use. The residential wing, with large glass façades, overlooks the surrounding landscape or gardens in the centre of the layout. The dining hall is fully enclosed, with high windows, lending the room a ceremonious, almost solemn air. The library has sun-screened windows, providing good light for the many reading desks but at the same time shielding the books from direct sunlight. St. Catherine's College is designed as an easily comprehended unit, but with rich nuancing of details and great variation in the design of individual rooms. Furniture, fittings, textiles and lighting were also designed by Arne Jacobsen. Some of the furniture was designed specially for St. Catherine's, but in simple and appropriate forms which enable it to be industrially produced. Jacobsen was also responsible for landscaping the garden and choosing the plants.

The development of industrial building was a disappointment to Arne Jacobsen. He saw it lead, in the majority of cases, to monotonous and expressionless buildings. And although he never abandoned his work of developing building systems and types suitable for industrial production, he tried for a time to apply the technological potentialities in more individual and more boldly designed buildings.

In the castle park of Herrenhausen in Hanover, in 1964, he designed a foyer for a concert hall accommodated in one of the old buildings. In association with this commission, he had been asked to design a viewing tower with a restaurant on the site of the bombed castle. From the restaurant it would be possible to view the entire park with its geometrically designed baroque beds. The building has never been finished, but the design is known to professionals all over the world. In association with Folmer Andersen, an engineer, Jacobsen designed the building as a large sculpture, to be despite its size, as unobtrusive as possible in this old setting. Restaurant and viewing platform were to be of steel space lattices with a thin cladding of, say, metal sheets. It is an organic design, rather like a mushroom, where, almost immediately, one also senses the lightness of the material.

In the same year, Jacobsen was commissioned to design a swimming stadium at Lyngby, north of Copenhagen. In this case again he collaborated with Folmer Andersen. The actual swimming hall was designed on a very original principle of construction, in which the roof is borne by six large girders, each consisting of seven prefabricated concrete components, clamped together by cables. Seven crossbeams are laid as shelves in the sloping girders, forming at the same time roof and recreational areas. Two of the shelves were envisaged as a restaurant, the others as open sunbathing sites. In the single-storey building which forms the base of the stadium's superstructure like a plateau are other bathing facilities and changing rooms.

The design has never been executed; unfortunately, because it would undoubtedly have been one of Arne Jacobsen's handsomest and most distinctive buildings.

In the 1960's, Jacobsen designed a large number of buildings abroad; an art gallery in Hanover, a town hall at Landskrona in Sweden, a bank in Kuwait, a town hall and other public buildings at Castrop-Rauxel, Germany, to name a few. Some had been abandoned before Jacobsen's death, while others were so far advanced that it will be possible to complete them in accordance with his ideas. The last building he helped to inaugurate was the first stage of the new National Bank of Denmark.

Arne Jacobsen's creativity and capacity for work remained undiminished till the end. At the time of his death he was working on the design of the first stage of a new university at Roskilde, west of Copenhagen. In this he was employing a building system, developed in his own drawing-room, of which he had great hopes. He had not abandoned his belief that industrialization could be applied without loss of architectural freedom.

He was also occupied till the end in developing new furniture designs and other articles for industrial production. Beauty and use for him were two aspects of the same thing, just as he combined work and experience in his own daily life. He turned everyday art into universal art.

Page 16-17

"The Egg and the Swan". Chairs designed for the firm of Fritz Hansen's Eftf., 1959.

Bellevue area in Klampenborg, north of Copenhagen.
Here Arne Jacobsen projected buildings for Bellevue beach, 1932; Bella Vista Apartments, 1933; Bellevue Theatre and Restaurant, 1934-35; Søholm chain and semi-detached housing development, 1950 and 1955; Bellevue Bay Apartments 1960-61. The Bella Vista building from 1932 is one of the first examples in Denmark of such multi-storeyed apartments designed along straight functional principles.

18

Town Hall in Søllerød, north of Copenhagen, 1940-42.
Designed in collaboration with Flemming Lassen, this civic centre is based on a suggestion which won first prize in a 1939 competition.
The building is of reinforced concrete with facades covered in light grey marble tile.

Søholm chain and semi-detached development, Klampenborg, 1950 and 1955. These homes are situated on the grounds of a former country estate. The development was plotted so that most of the precious old trees could be preserved. The houses are of yellow brick with roofs in dark asbestos cement slate. All offer a view over the Øresund, the picturesque strait separating Denmark and Sweden. This view takes in the garden of the Arne Jacobsen residence in Søholm.

Munkegaard School, Gentofte, 1952-56.
A grade school for children aged 7 to 15,
Munkegaard School has all regular classrooms in single-storey buildings so that
each class can have its own courtyard
garden. The landscaping was planned by
Arne Jacobsen to give each courtyard a
characteristic shape with flagstone place-
ment and plant arrangement different
from all the others.
Special classrooms are situated in a long
two-storey wing. There is a spacious
auditorium at the hub. Yellow brick was
selected as the structural material, and
the design is carried right into the class-
room interiors where untreated yellow
brick walls lend a bright, clean effect.
Arne Jacobsen himself designed the
furnishings, down to tables, chairs,
lamps, curtains, and the auditorium stage
curtain.

Rødovre Town Hall, west of Copenhagen, 1955.

This town hall in a fast-growing suburb is actually two buildings: a three-storey administration centre and a council meeting hall. A corridor connects the two units. The town hall marks the beginning of a period in which Arne Jacobsen created an architectonic medium suitable for incorporating prefabricated components. Thus this reinforced concrete structure is designed on the cantilever principle, with all the load at the center of the building, allowing a lightweight pre-cast curtain-wall to be hung from the supporting concrete overhang.

Rødovre Town Hall

SAS Royal Hotel and Air Terminal, Copenhagen, 1958-60.
Copenhagen's first skyscraper comprises a low horizontal building, housing an air terminal and a hotel foyer, topped by a soaring block of hotel rooms and attendant facilities.
The building is clad with a curtain-wall of aluminium and glass. Its facade is like a huge mirror that reflects the surroundings so that the building takes on the hue and feel of its milieu.
Again, Arne Jacobsen designed his hotel's interior appointments so that furniture, textiles, lighting, and every detail blend in one great concept. The foyer is brightened with indirect daylight from an indoor winter garden that rises through two floors.

Head office for the Hamburg Power Station, 1970.
This big administration building was projected in cooperation with Otto Weitling on the basis of a suggestion which won first prize in an international competition. The high-rise structures, which hold the administration offices, rest on a low horizontal base containing public facilities, service offices, conference rooms and staff cafeterias.

St. Catherine's College, Oxford, 1964-66. In accordance with English tradition, the buildings are placed around a quadrangle. In other respects there is little sign of tradition. The structural elements are of prefabricated reinforced concrete. Two long wings, which mark the boundaries of this installation, contain the student residences. Three larger buildings along the axis house the dining area, library and auditoriums.

Page 36-37
Design for a lookout tower and restaurant in Herrenhaus Park, Hanover, 1964.
Herrenhaus Castle was destroyed during World War II. The park is a well preserved baroque garden with an ornate, elaborate shape that is seen to best advantage from above. On the site where the castle stood, therefore, the plan was to build a lookout platform and restaurant. Arne Jacobsen's concept, never brought to reality, envisages a great sculptural work as little reminiscent of a traditional building as possible, and which therefore would not invoke memories of the baroque castle that once commanded the park.

Design for a swimming stadium in Lyng-by, north of Copenhagen, 1964.
This project, as yet unrealized, is one of Arne Jacobsen's most original works. Like the lookout tower in Herrenhaus, the constructive idea here is clearly expressed in the form. These two projects were conceived in close collaboration with M. Folmer Andersen.

The National Bank of Denmark, Copenhagen, 1971.
Invited to submit a plan in competition with other architects, Arne Jacobsen was awarded the project of new buildings for his country's National Bank. The first stage of the structure to house, among other operations, a note printing plant, was inaugurated just before the architect's death. The second stage, with the spacious bank hall, will commence in 1972.

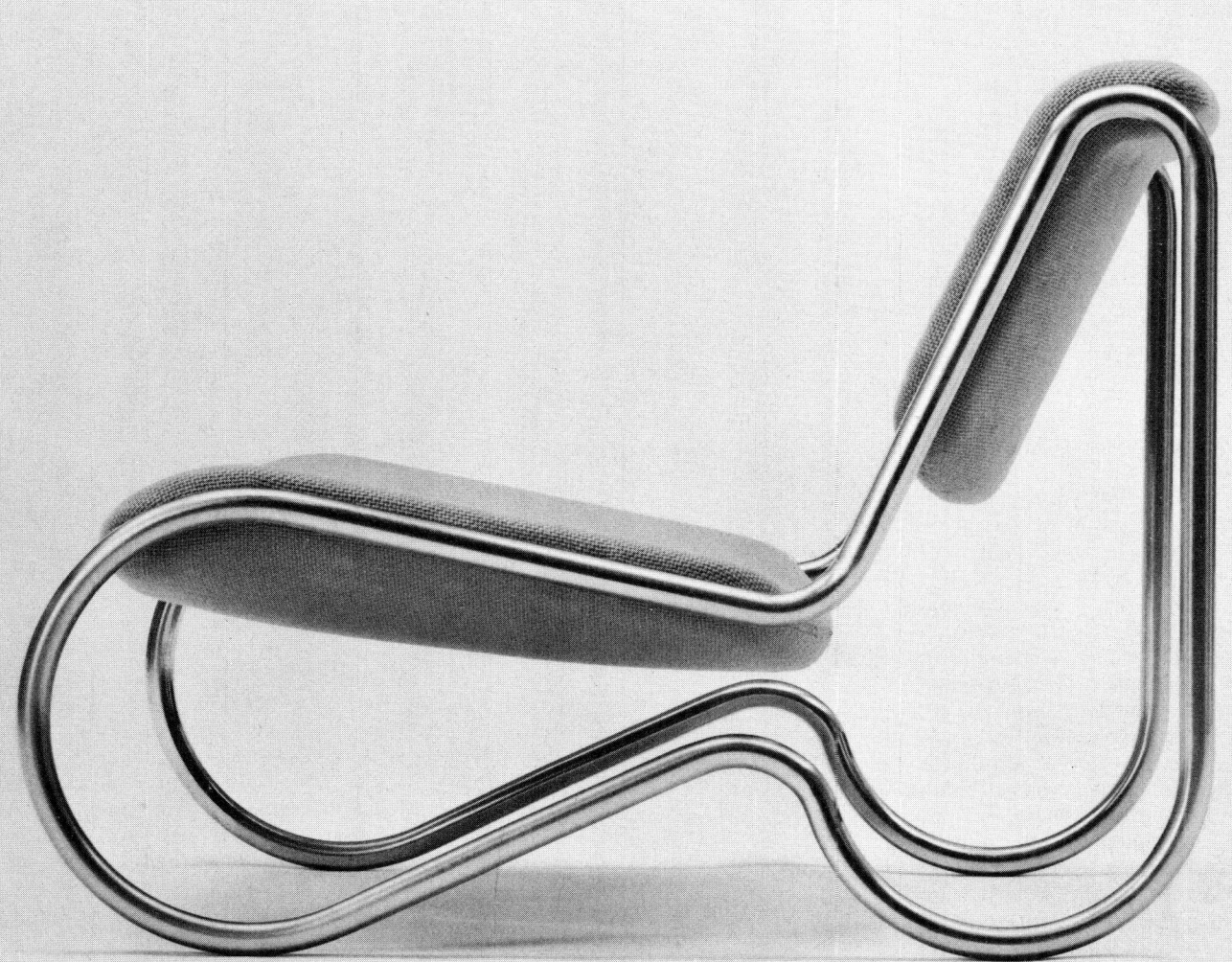

Page 40-41
One of Arne Jacobsen's last designs:
Easy-chairs in tubular steel and moulded
polyether which can be combined to form
a sofa. Manufactured by Fritz Hansen's
Eftf. A/S.

Stacking chairs, designed for the firm
of Fritz Hansen's Eftf.
In 1952, Arne Jacobsen designed a chair
with seat and back moulded from a single
piece of laminated veneer. The chair had
three legs of light steel tubing. Designed
for mass production, it became an ex-
tremely popular and much exported chair.
Later, Arne Jacobsen developed new
models on the same principle and a se-
ries of variants in different kinds of wood,
lacquered in various colours or covered
with fabric or leather. With additions to
the fundamental type, these stacking
chairs have been adapted for a number
of different purposes – for auditorium
use, as church chairs, and for use aboard
ships. Today this kind of chair is found
all over the world, in private homes and
many kinds of institutions.

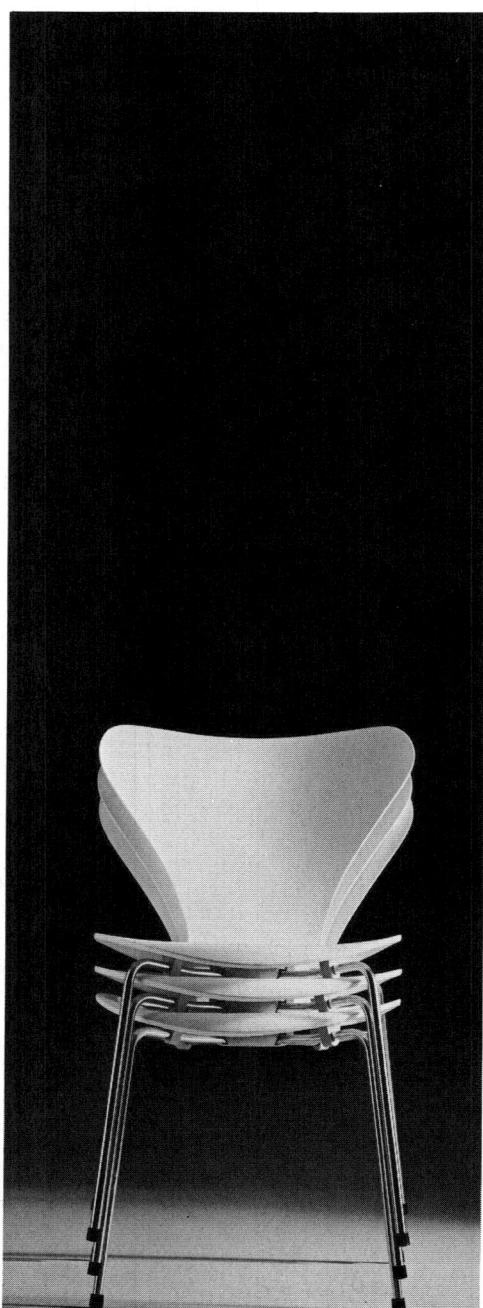

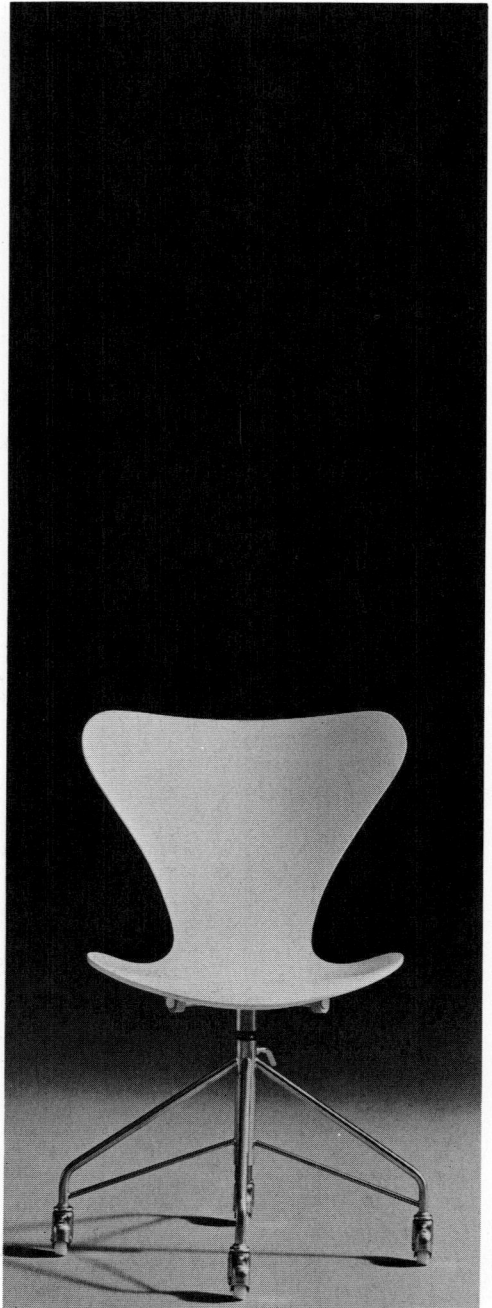

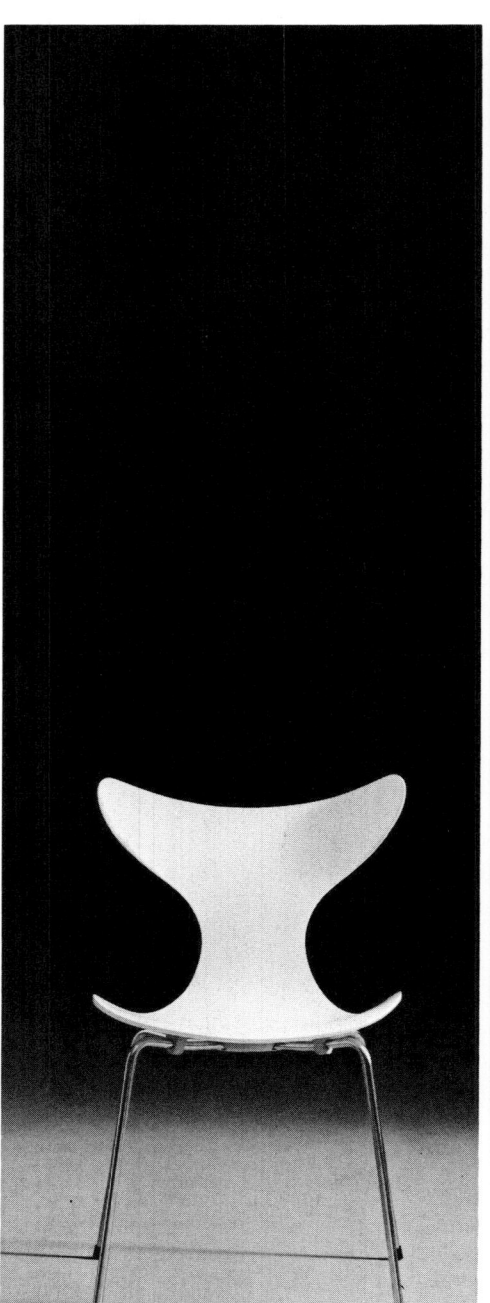
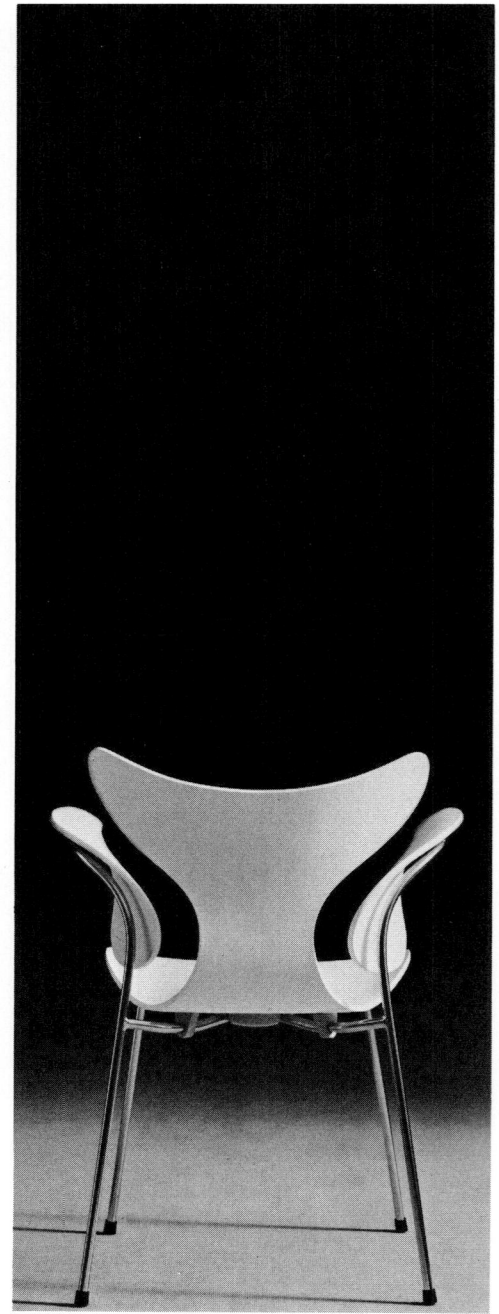

44

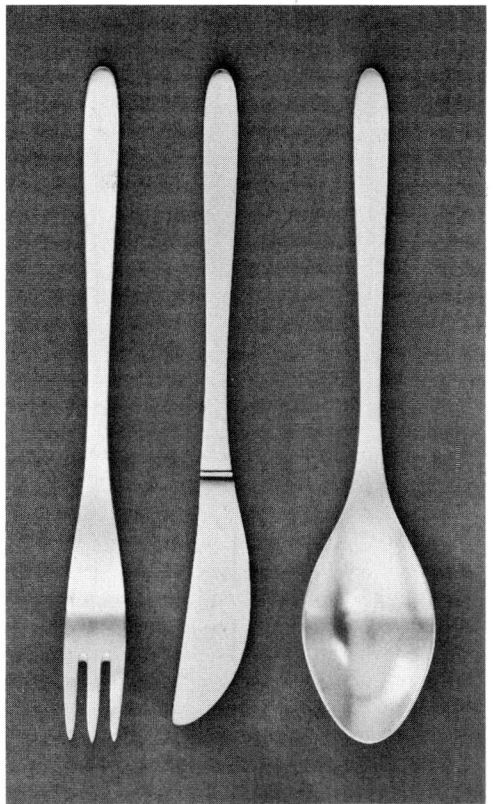

Eating utensils and tableware of stainless steel.

Among the many utilitarian objects Arne Jacobsen created are flatware for court jeweller A. Michelsen and a line of stainless tableware known as 'Cylinda Line', and designed for Stelton A/S. These examples of mass-produced articles show how, with proper design, a standard of quality can be attained that rivals far more expensive, handmade articles.

The new is always criticized

Arne Jacobsen on creative activity, pastries, neighbourliness, imagination, his country, parents, art, architecture and scented roses . . .

Interviews with Arne Jacobsen were rare in the Danish Press, but when the first stage of the National Bank's new building in Copenhagen, one of the architect's last completed works, was inaugurated in the spring of 1971 the Copenhagen newspaper *Politiken* published this interview on February 25. The interviewer was Anne Wolden-Ræthinge, who has specialized in profile interviews, for which she is one of the best-known Danish journalists. The interview is translated from *Politiken* in full and unedited.

Arne Jacobsen was a talented photographer.

46

A curly little fluff of wool is picked up meticulously from the carpet. A rolled-up drawing is removed from the otherwise uncluttered desk. All is spick and span. On the wall, Richard Mortensen's atmospheric blue lines and Robert Jacobsen's airily flowing iron sculpture lift the room into space.

On light steps the master enters the door; even the acoustics suggest that this man builds in heights.

Or is it because Arne Jacobsen is successfully approaching journey's end of a zealous slimming cure? 'Have one of my home-made pastries; it's all because I've been put on this damned slimming diet that I've got so good at giving things away. Only keep all this private chit-chat out of it; I think a man's private life is what he shares with his wife and children and grandchildren, according to his age. It seems to me that most popular magazines get produced on the basis of that; and I don't think it has anything to do with love of one's fellow men, I think it's just idle curiosity. I don't think that it enlarges our interest in one another. The well-to-do lady dispensing recipes as she waters flowers: what good is that to good neighbourliness?

'If ever I read personal material – biographies – it's only when it has something to do with my job – you'll soon discover that I'm a bit of a one-track specialist. And that's rather saddening; for one often feels strangely clipped, not having time to burble, though one actually has many interests. Architecture seems to absorb everything else; it's become one's entire life.

'But one does, of course, make architecture for one's fellow men; they are the ones that are going to use it. On the other hand, there are many who accuse me of not paying enough regard to my fellow-men; and one is a party to the case, so one can't judge, and occasionally I say to myself: "I wonder if they're right?" One can nearly always see a thing from two sides, if only one has a little imagination. It's so devilish hard to be clearcut; both sides can be right, and then you're described as unsure. Hasn't one a right to be? Isn't it very natural? I sympathize with the politicians for having to take clearcut decisions and seem mighty sure . . .

'They always say: "That's clear . . ."'

'I'm not a sociologist, I'm only an architect. One of the things now taking place at the Academy is that sociology and psychology are being enthroned, and I regard that as fine – so long as young people don't take so great an interest in these subjects as to forget to build a house. Because architecture is knowing technology and a sensitiveness to the artistic side of the matter. People talk so much today about building further on things themselves and achieving the wellbeing they are after: the door-to-door method and all the stuff your paper is full of every day. And then we have found that at Albertslund, for instance, hardly anybody has availed himself of these opportunities; they scarcely know how to arrange a sunny spot in their garden. And this is where I feel a bit nervous about what could give people a meaning to their lives, what they could build further on, which is imagination – and I don't think people are overburdened with that.

'Every time I build a house it's consigned to hell by some people. In 1934, when Stelling House was finished, the paper said I should be banned from building for life. When the SAS building was inaugurated, a paper sponsored a competition to select the ugliest house in the city – I won the first prize. And Erik Møller and I had another awful to-do over Århus Town Hall.

'Yes, of course, one is saddened by this; because the criticism nearly always comes where something new appears

and you want to get it out. And though one doesn't make such heavy weather over an ordinary reader's letter as over a contribution from a professional, one realizes that the letter was written by somebody involved enough to sit down and write it and post it, and many really serious things come out in readers' letters and give rise to debate. It's a proof of freedom, and I suppose that it's that that one sets highest.'

'*Do you feel a little bit like the prophet without honour in his own country?*'

'Obviously, the country one belongs to feels the greatest right to criticize one. Actually, there's nothing wrong in that.'

'*Have your international commissions never tempted you to settle abroad?*'

'I tried to be a refugee in Sweden, where indeed I was happy, but seemed to get overcome occasionally by a cheap sentimentality which told me that I ought not to live abroad.'

'*In what architectural setting was your childhood passed?*'

'It was in a flat; but as my parents were rather old I was a bit too lively for them, and so I was sent to boarding school at Nærum, and that was a happy time for me. It was a place where you learnt to enthuse about nature, and the food we got was quite fantastically good, considerably better than the teaching staff, as one discovered later. But it may well be that that's why I'm having to diet now; one's stomach was distended in childhood, and so it takes a lot to fill it now. When I was awarded a silver medal for a chair, in Paris in 1925, I was sent the programme, where it said "artist Arne Jacobsen". But my father said: "That must be a mistake, my boy: you're no artist and you're too fat to be an artiste."

'*But you weren't deterred by paternal scepticism?*'

'Of course one was sorry in one's heart, but it has meant that one has become armed to the teeth, in order to fight to make something decent. I painted my room white; my parents thought that was completely barbarous – on top of the expensive wallpaper with the coloured pattern! But I think that parents who criticize their children too much are in fact better than parents who praise their children too much. Incidentally, I think that when one has been through a boarding school, especially then, you have some resistance; because it was both fine comradeship and a fairly hard training.'

'*Was it your father, too, who jogged the palette out of your hand?*'

'Old Vilhelm Wanscher once took some of my sketches from the school of architecture and said: "I'll hang these at the school of painting, as that's where they belong!" ... Yes, it was again my father ... But when I'm travelling I draw and paint sketches which are great fun to sit with. And when you're fully aware that it has nothing to do with art, I think that's all right.'

'*But architecture is art.*'

'If building becomes architecture, then it is an art. Clearly, if a building is not functionally and technically in order, then it isn't architecture either, it's only building. It has been said for many years that when a thing is practical and functional, it is beautiful as well. That I don't believe, because there are different ways of solving a problem functionally – without ever managing to be beautiful! If architecture didn't have to do with art, it would be astonishingly easy to build houses, but the architect's task – his most difficult task – is always that of selecting. When you have a problem to solve there are nearly always different solutions – many times many solutions, sometimes only a few solutions – and they may all of them be practical and functional. But they may lack the aesthetic solution which raises the result to architecture. That's where the artistic comes in: in selecting the best of these solutions.

'Unfortunately, I don't possess the ability to see the obvious solution immediately. I don't feel sure until I've confronted my first solution with other solutions; that it is so often the first solution which turns out to be the right one is another matter. But inspiration? That's when you come home from abroad and are asked: "Well, have you found inspiration?" and fortunately you haven't ... But the impressions sink in, of course, and emerge perhaps later: none of us has invented the house; that was done many thousands of years ago.'

'*What does the architectural idea of beauty consist of?*'

'The primary factor is the proportional. It is precisely the proportions which make the old Greek temples classic in their beauty. They are like great blocks, from which the air has been literally hewn out between the columns. And whether one looks at a building from the Baroque, the Renaissance or today, those one wants to look at, those one admires, are all well-proportioned; that is vital. Next comes the material, not mixing wrong materials together. And out of that comes of course the colour – and together the overall impression.

'*You will soon be going to receive a prize from the French Academy. Is that one's real reward?*'

'No, the vital thing is to see things grow; to start with a small sketch and see the whole and the details become reality. It may sound a bit affected; but it is the actual creative activity, whether it's a teaspoon or a national bank. For there always comes a time when one, as it were, feels one's lack of skill, feels doubt. To get a thing realized; to get it where one can say "There, now it's good"; that's very difficult to achieve. Many a time one sets oneself high aims. Perhaps too high.

'*Does it pain you to see one of your own*

houses dolled up with frilly, lace curtains?'

'Not pain – but I just don't understand it. I remember one of my workmen saying to me once: "Look, Mr. Jacobsen, it's not nice of you to call the wife's curtains baggy bloomers!" And I was sorry because he loved both his wife and her curtains. At that moment I realized I had overstepped my authority.'

'Is good taste out in this country?'

'Now I can't stand the term "good taste"; as if we were talking about ladies' hats. I would rather say: artistic approach, receptiveness, alertness. In one way the sense of quality has got better; the status symbol in little things has gone; people will presume to have stainless steel, even though the neighbours have silver. I readily think that prefabrication and industrial design make people more neighbourly. I think that's a good thing. On the other hand, I don't understand the enthusiasm for everything in the antique shop that Grandma threw out. There I think the sense of quality has declined; otherwise Grandma wouldn't have thrown it out. But here in Denmark where we are so democratic, we use the little phrase "it's a matter of taste" of both pastry and architecture.'

'And you eat only architect-designed pastry?'

'Pastry usually tastes best when it looks nice. A custard flap, surely that looks nice. In fact there's nothing I don't mind if it looks nice.

'Are you thinking of retirement?'

'Not if my health holds out; I hope to see the National Bank finished in six-seven years' time. Otherwise I'd no doubt cultivate my garden; I shall end up as the old gardener. Up to now I've been most fond of foliage plants that flower, but in which flowering is not the most important. I've never really cared much for roses; there's something flashy and assertive about modern roses, and I think it's a pity they haven't any scent. But now I've found a nurseryman who has spent forty years of his life cultivating roses with a scent; flat-shaped roses like the old Dutch paintings. They are really tremendously beautiful; I grow them in the garden of my summer cottage.'

'Do you never spend your big fees on luxury?'

'We have never lived grandly or in style; and one reason for that is that, although at times I may have made money I have always had the feeling that you can't go on doing it, and so why should you have the upset of having a high standard of living reduced to a more sensible one?'

Toms Chocolate factory in Ballerup, 1961.

Working with Arne Jacobsen
By Alan Bullock
Master of St. Catherine's College and Vice Chancellor of the University of Oxford

The first time I came across the name of Arne Jacobsen I was turning the pages of an architectural journal in search of an architect for a new college which we were founding at Oxford. Our willingness to look abroad for an architect surprised many people and stirred up a storm of controversy before we had finished. But the great burst of university building which marked the 1960's in Britain had not yet begun and I felt no conviction in looking at the buildings we visited that a British architect would have the self-confidence to stand up to the pressures of tradition in a place like Oxford and strike a balance between creating something which would be so out of keeping with the rest that it would never be accepted as an Oxford college and producing an imitation which would fail to establish a distinctive identity of its own. We were, in fact, searching for an architect who could grasp and express that identity for us, before it had yet taken clear shape in our own minds.

We must have looked at several hundred pages of photographs and plans, and I made a long trip round the U.S.A. to see the best of America's modern architecture. However, the severe, simple lines of the Jacobsen building I had seen in the journal remained clearly fixed in my memory and when we decided to visit Scandinavia, his name was on the short list of architects whose work we most wanted to see.

I had the advantage of examining all Arne Jacobsen's buildings before I met the man himself, so that we were able to form an impression of his work without being influenced, one way or the other, by his personality. On the ground, it was possible to answer a question which photographs had failed to settle, whether the austerity of Jacobsen's style – the unbroken straight lines, the absence of any ornament or relief, the simple geometrical proportions – produced an impression of impersonality and coldness or of humanity and warmth. One look at Munkegaard School was enough to satisfy me: I have never seen a school more perfectly fitted – in its scale, in the use of materials and colour, and in the planting of its courtyards – to make a child feel at home in it. From the moment I walked into Munkegaards School, I felt convinced that after nearly two years of looking we had found the architect we wanted.

Nobody we talked to in Denmark was at all surprised that we should think so highly of Arne Jacobsen's work, they thought the same; but when it came to asking what sort of a man he was to work with, then our Danish friends shrugged their shoulders and shook their heads uncertainly – we must see him and make up our minds for ourselves. They were unwilling to say more, but he had the reputation of being difficult.

When I came to know Arne Jacobsen, I thought this reputation was undeserved. I never found him a difficult man to work with, but I understood why some people thought so. An English architect who admired his work said to me, in an outburst of exasperation, "What he won't see is that the role of the architect has changed, that in these days of technology and mass production, he cannot afford to be a perfectionist or to think of himself as an artist. Jacobsen hasn't even got a proper drawing office, he wants to do everything himself and to design every single thing in his buildings, furniture, gardens, the lot. Such individualism is impossible in the modern world." As a general proposition, this may be true, but when it came to our particular building (and no client is ever interested in more than this), I looked on such qualities in an architect as the highest recommendation.

When we finally got Jacobsen to visit Oxford, it soon became clear that the

question was, not whether we should appoint him, but whether he would accept the appointment if we offered it to him. He would undertake no commission, however attractive, unless he was convinced that he could produce a solution which would satisfy him. This may have been one of the reasons for his reputation as a "difficult" man to work with, but it was not a pose and I soon came to see Jacobsen's "difficult" side as an expression of the personal quality I most admired in him – his integrity, which in practice meant a refusal to accept second-best solutions or to compromise with his own high standards.

This could lead to trouble, especially when the budget was tight, for the materials and the quality of "finish" Jacobsen demanded were expensive. But this was where he showed his resourcefulness. Three times out of four, when we had reached a deadlock between what the building committee wanted (or thought the college could afford) and what the architect thought essential, Jacobsen would come back the next day with a quite new proposal. He did not compromise, but looked for another, unexpected way out of the impasse. When we pulled his sketch plans across the table and tried to indicate how a design could be modified, he would roll them up and say, "Please don't try to improve it. It is much better to say that you do not like what I have proposed. Then, tomorrow, I will produce something different." And instead of a compromise, a watered down version of an original idea, he would start again with a completely new proposal, often radically different in character.

I don't think Jacobsen could stop designing. When we took him to a warehouse to choose the kitchen equipment, he spent most of the time re-designing what he saw on scraps of paper. My only regret was that we had not got half a million pounds more so that we could really have given him his head. Even within our limited budget we commissioned him to design not only the buildings of the college, but all the furniture, table silver, light fittings, curtains, everything down to the ash trays and bronze door handles. This was the way to get the best out of him. He had the imagination and the skill to carry out a total design, to create a world of his own. For eight years now I have lived in that world, the world of Arne Jacobsen, and still take delight in it. Far from feeling that he imposed his taste on me, I felt and still feel that my eyes were opened for the first time to so much that I had failed to see before.

My education had been a literary and historical one; I had never been taught to use my eyes or to pay more than perfunctory attention to the quality of the environment in which I lived. Simply by watching Arne Jacobsen at work – for he rarely talked about his work and had a great distrust of theorising about architecture – I received a second, visual education at the hands of a master of modern design, as exciting an experience as if I had suddenly learned to speak a new language and found that I could understand what people were saying in Chinese.

This process still continues. Arne Jacobsen took as deep – and informed – an interest in the natural, living forms of plants as he did in the shapes of buildings and furniture. At our invitation he planned the gardens of the college with every shrub and tree placed so that it would form a part of the architectural design. If he had his way, he told me, nobody would be allowed to live in the college for ten years after the builders had left, so as to give Nature time to establish a unity between the buildings and their setting. Every year I have watched his happening, watched the almost imperceptible process by which his buildings have "settled" into the landscape and realised that this was a part of his design. In the very week he died I noticed – after looking without noticing for several years – that the plants which he chose to fill the brick panels along the wall of the college hall will eventually, when they reach full height, give the effect of green pillars.

Any man who is a perfectionist can except to meet a great deal of frustration, doubly so if he is an architect and so dependent not only on clients, committees and their budgets but also on manufacturers, building contractors, subcontractors and their labour force. Every building must have fallen short of what he knew it could be like, but Jacobsen never gave up trying to get perfection. He did this quietly, without making scenes, and by the time I knew him had acquired an authority, again quietly expressed, which few people ever contested except on grounds of expense. As a man, he was reserved: there were areas fenced off which no one was allowed to enter. The two of us got on well, enjoyed smoking our pipes and shared many laughs together. I took my family to Denmark and visited his home – he was wonderful with children and spent hours with us in Tivoli – and of course he was in and out of my house in Oxford. I suppose I was as close to him as any client ever was, but he kept me at a distance and I respected this. Only his wife, I believe, knew the inner man for although he had a natural charm, he did not like social occasions, was impatient of small talk and did all he could to avoid publicity. No man did less to promote himself and when recognition came, rather belatedly, he was as much embarrassed as pleased by it. From first to last the most difficult critic he had to satisfy was himself, and if *he* was satisfied I do not think he cared much what the critics thought or said. On his visits to Oxford, he liked best of all to slip off on his own and wander round the city with a camera, spending his time looking at buildings, at old furniture, at plants and gardens. His eyes were insatiable and in this way he discovered all sorts of odd beauties which we, who lived in the place, had never noticed. A conversation with him, at least in English, a language which he protested he could not speak, invariably ended with a pencil sketch to illustrate what he meant, and attempts to draw him out on aesthetic questions or discussion of architecture got nowhere. He expressed himself not in words but in design, and in design few of our contemporaries have said more perfectly what they wanted to say. St. Catherine's was only one of many buildings by which Arne Jacobsen will be remembered, and anyone who wants to see the full range of his achievement must visit Denmark. He had too many ideas ever to be in danger of repeating himself, but I am certain that I could recognise one of his buildings anywhere. For everything he built has the same classical quality – simplicity of design, reliance upon proportions, the absence of ornament or fussy detail, purity of line. Shortly before he died Jacobsen was asked by a correspondent of *The Times* which of his buildings he had enjoyed most and replied, St. Catherine's. All I can say is that our partnership with Arne Jacobsen in creating St. Catherine's was one of the decisive, as it was certainly one of the most exciting experiences of my life. It was he who gave this new college its distinctive identity by providing it with buildings and a setting in which, the longer I live in them, the more I find to delight and satisfy me.

Arne Jacobsen – a Danish architect.
Published by the Danish Ministry of
Foreign Affairs, Press and Cultural
Relations Department, Christiansborg
Castle, DK-1218 Copenhagen K.
This book is published as a New Year
greeting 1971/72 and is not for sale.
Editor: Søren Dyssegaard
Layout: Freddy Kring
Photos: Strüwing, Mydtskov and Rønne,
Arne Jacobsen.
Translation: Reginald Spink and
Bodil Garner
Printed by Vang Rasmussen's
Lithographic Printing House, Copenhagen.
ISBN 87 85112 00 3